C000186307

ISBN 978-0-666-24441-3
PIBN 10579457

English
Français
Deutsche
Italiano
Español
Português

www.forgottenbooks.com

Mythology Photography **Fiction**
Fishing Christianity **Art** Cooking
Essays Buddhism Freemasonry
Medicine **Biology** Music **Ancient
Egypt** Evolution Carpentry Physics
Dance Geology **Mathematics** Fitness
Shakespeare **Folklore** Yoga Marketing
Confidence Immortality Biographies
Poetry **Psychology** Witchcraft
Electronics Chemistry History **Law**
Accounting **Philosophy** Anthropology
Alchemy Drama Quantum Mechanics
Atheism Sexual Health **Ancient History**
Entrepreneurship Languages Sport
Paleontology Needlework Islam
Metaphysics Investment Archaeology
Parenting Statistics Criminology
Motivational

ana ian o 1e y

for the

ec ion o   1r

Incorporated under the Ontario Companies Act
Toronto, January 28th, 1915

REPORT

Secretary, Miss L. B. Durand, and of the
Acting Treasurer, Mr. T. H. Barton,
for the year 1918

AND

Report of the Secretary, Miss L. B. Durand,
and of the Treasurer, Mr. C. H. Anderson,
for the year 1919

> "The robins know the melting snow;
> The sparrow meek, prophetic-eyed,
> Her nest beside the snow-drift weaves,
> Secure the osier yet will hide
> Her callow brood in mantling leaves.—
> And thou, by science all undone,
> Why only must thy reason fail
> To see the southing of the sun?"

153 UNIVERSITY AVENUE, TORONTO

REPORT OF THE SECRETARY OF THE
CANADIAN SOCIETY FOR THE PROTECTION OF BIRDS
read at the Annual Meeting and Luncheon in the
King Edward Hotel, December 31, 1918.

In submitting my report I would say that the past year has been the most anxious and trying for the Secretary since incorporation, the resultant gloom and shortcomings arising from several causes, but not in ourselves. We are still carrying on, and foresee a vast number of people in Canada, not necessarily connected with this organization, though possibly inspired by its efforts, zealous as we are for the protection of birds.

While it would be more effective were efforts unified, we are, neverthe-less, mightily pleased at the efforts of others, since such an extension ful-fills the ends of our being.

Your Secretary is deeply grateful for the continued confidence of many members, some of whom are here to-day, who have upheld this effort since that memorable night of December 16, 1914, when they inscribed their names on the application of the new-born Society for a charter of service to the community. The war was at that time in its earliest stage of raging and has raged up to within a few weeks ago, and absorbed the energies of numbers of people who in normal times would have welcomed and gener-ously supported the objects which the Society has in view.

Some of our members went to the front; others dropped out in order to devote themselves more exclusively to war work. A few who did neither attempted to discourage our enterprise by slights, misrepresentation, fault-finding, trouble-making, and, in one case, by genuine Hunnish frightfulness. These, we understand, are incident to all public service and common experi-ences in organizing and conducting any social work, however disinterested-ly. "Just human nature," philosophic friends assure us.

The work of the year has been handicapped by the loss of our Treas-urer, who had hardly got into harness when he resigned.

As this event occurred on the eve of the Baynes' lecture, and when the Secretary was elsewhere occupied, the Treasurer's resignation was a mis-fortune. Nevertheless, with the assistance of Dr. Clarke, Mr. Fraser, Mr. Payne, Mr. Barton and others, the sale of tickets was successful and the expenses of the lecture were about covered. As will be seen from the Treasurer's report, Mr. Baynes' charges were most moderate. His lecture on "How to Attract Wild Birds," given with one hundred excellent original lantern slides, in the Greek Temple, North St., on April 4th, was the best ever delivered in Toronto, both in the scientific and popular aspects. Mr. Baynes delighted us all by the fullness and exactness of his information and his enthusiasm for his subject. The engagement of Mr. Baynes was effected at the request of Mr. C. G. Fraser, and the lecture took place, especially for the advantage of the delegates of the O. E. A., as the date was most inopportune for this Society which, by some misunderstanding, bore the entire expense. However, but a few weeks ago, Mr. Fraser learned that an appropriation of one hundred dollars had been made by the Department of Education to cover the expense of the lecture, and this amount was in due course transferred to the exchequer of the Society and relieved its financial crisis.

On April 16th, the executive appointed Mr. T. H. Barton to be Acting Treasurer, with the assistance of the Secretary. But the fees of only a few members had been collected and the funds in hand did not warrant any extension of the work during the spring and summer of 1918.

The Secretary, meanwhile, sought channels of service entailing no financial outlay and negotiated with the editor of the Presbyterian Publications, Rev. Dr. R. D. Fraser, for assistance and space in the columns of his junior periodicals in which to present the cause of the birds to children. Dr. Fraser cordially assented to the proposition and in the earliest possible numbers, in October (1918) of The King's Own, printed an invitation to its readers to become junior members of this Association on payment of 10 cents for pin, literature, membership card and return postage. This amount does not cover the cost of the returns given to the children, which must be supplemented from the general funds. But the value of what is given is enhanced by making a small charge. As the result of these efforts the Association has enrolled several hundred junior members from all parts of Canada, and the interest is extending.

In September your Secretary planned an entertainment for the children of Toronto, and enlisted the interest of Mr. W. D. Hobson, Woodstock, who generously consented to give a lecture on birds and their calls, in Convocation Hall on the 25th of that month, his railway expenses only being paid. Mr. Otto James, organist of the Church of the Redeemer, consented to give several selections on the organ, with Mr. Moure's approval, to add to the pleasure of the children. The response to our invitation was only too enthusiastic, thousands of persons attending. The hall proved too large for the volume of woodland bird calls, and, the audience becoming restless, the programme could not be carried out fully. A large number of children, however, evinced interest in the bird specimens and a few enlisted in bird protection. Mr. Barton kindly occupied the chair and entertained Mr. Hobson as his guest.

For many weeks following this event influenza was epidemic in Toronto, and a ban was laid on all meetings. But at the very earliest opportunity your Secretary organized a second lecture by Mr. Hobson, which was delivered in Forresters' Hall on November 19, the reserved seats being sold at 50 cents and general admission being 25 cents. This lecture was greatly enjoyed by all those so wise as to be present, Mr. Hobson being one of the best bird men in Canada and possessing a unique repertoire of bird calls.

The Treasurer's report will show that none of these lectures netted the Directors anything but the interest awakened, or kept alive, in bird life, and the approval of their own consciences for their efforts in behalf of the Association.

Miss Peggy Howell, with Chickadee

During the past year we have lost by their death two life members and several annual members. Mrs. Lila Cameron, Meaford, Ont., was a charter life member. She died in August. Last February we lost one of our kindest friends in Mr. L. Clark Macklem. The very last meeting he attended prior to his long illness was a general meeting of this Association, held in our office, on November 5th (1917). Miss Jessie Rounthwaite, an annual member, died last winter, and Clayton Duff, our charter member in Bluevale, Ont., died April 24th of this year (1918). Clayton Duff was a Canadian hero, bound during all his life of 34 years to a bed or a wheel chair, yet surging with mental energy, and the desire for service. He practically organized Bluevale for the birds. I doubt if anyone in the village would injure a bird, if only out of love for him, and a large number of its children are enrolled as members of this Association. One of Clayton Duff's friends, the Canadian poet Ethelwyn Wetherald, has enshrined his memory in some affectionate lines which appeared in "The Welland Telegraph," and are as follows:

"Lover of children, flowers and birds,
Of artist vision and poet words;

Weaver of joys from threads of pain,
Changer of loss into highest gain;

Maker of picture, poem and jest,
From days of weariness, nights of unrest;

Pining for spring and the bluebird's call,
Yet giving a bird-like bliss to us all;

Clayton Duff, we breathe your name
With tears and smiles and a sense of shame

That we who had everything life could give
Had to learn from you how best to live.

Goodbye! The memory of your ways
Gives lasting radiance to our days.

For from your bed—almost a grave—
You made it easier to be brave.

Another of our most active yet shut-in members is Miss Effie Lafferty, a patient in St. Joseph's Hospital, Chatham, who, though always reclining, uses her eyes and field glasses with extraordinary success, and observes a great number of species at all seasons in the grounds of the Hospital. In a letter, dated October 10, 1918, she writes:

"I thought I had found a new sparrow last month. It was a rather different shape, seemed very tame and came up close beside me in the lodge. I got all its points and when I came back to my room a wild hunt ensued to identify my bird. It was a rather crest-fallen bird-lover who had to conclude that her strange new bird was but a moulting song sparrow."

A general meeting of members was held on November 29th last, in the Ornithological room of the Reference Library, College St., through the courtesy of the Chief Librarian, Dr. Locke. On that occasion the following notices of motion of amendment of the constitution were read, which will to-day be presented for your approval:—

Mrs. L. Clark Macklem gave Notice of Motion of an amendment of the

Constitution to provide for the election of Patrons on their payment of $100 at any one time to the Society's funds, and the election of Benefactors on their payment of $1,000 at any one time to the Society's funds, the names of Patrons and Benefactors to be printed on letterheads, reports, leaflets, etc., issued by the Association.

Miss Durand gave Notice of Motion for the immediate printing of the Constitution of this Association, with provisions for the organization of Junior Clubs.

Mrs. MacFarlane gave Notice of Motion of an amendment to the Constitution providing for the appointment of Honorary Presidents, Honorary Vice-Presidents, and Provincial Vice-Presidents, in the persons of those prominently interested in the protection of birds, to hold office for one year, with re-appointment at the discretion of the executive.

The continued prevalence of influenza and the absence of our President from town have delayed the date of our annual meeting until the last day of the year. The Directors, however, have not been idle in the interval and organized a deputation to wait upon the Hon. G. F. Macdiarmid, Minister of Public Works, to ask for a grant. The following took part: Mr. Barton, Mrs. L. Clark Macklem, Mrs. L. A. Spaulding, Mrs. F. T. James, Miss Barbara Ewan, Miss Durand, Mr. Chester B. Hamilton, Mr. J. D. Spence, Mr. Payne and Dr. Powell. The Minister received the members cordially and listened attentively to their remarks.

Mr. T. Herbert Barton, who headed the deputation, said:

The Canadian Society for the Protection of Birds was founded a few years ago by Miss Durand for the purpose of encouraging the protection of our insectivorous birds, and notwithstanding the war our membership has steadily increased until at the present time we have an adult membership of over 300, and a junior membership of several thousand, extending over the whole Dominion.

The junior members are admitted to membership without payment of a fee, but a charge of ten cents is made for the bird pin, which is forwarded by post. This sum does not in fact defray the expense of procuring and mailing the pins, but we are very anxious to reach the children and make known to them the value of our birds and the large numbers of insects and weed seeds destroyed by them each year. In this way we are endeavoring to induce the children to protect bird life, for it is well known that most boys (in the country at any rate) carry small fire arms and do not miss an opportunity of exhibiting their skill at shooting small birds. If the children learn of the great advantages to be gained by protecting instead of destroying the birds, we feel quite satisfied that the practice will cease.

Our publicity campaign is being carried on through the medium of the Sunday School periodicals, and without charge to us.

Up to the present time our Secretary, Miss Durand, has given a large part of her time voluntarily to the work of our Society but this work occasioned by the increase of our junior membership has now reached such proportions that it is impossible to thus handle it. We are desirous of employing a permanent Secretary who can be in attendance at the office and look after the ever-increasing correspondence.

As we are carrying on a work of National importance, we feel we are justified in asking the Government for an annual grant of $1,000.00 to help defray these expenses.

We cannot properly continue our work without it. While we have an adult membership of over 300 who are supposed to pay an annual fee of $1.00 each, we have not been able to collect all the fees, and even if the fees were all paid, we would still have a large deficit.

While our junior membership embraces the whole Dominion, the majority of our members are children living in Ontario. They are taking a great interest in the work of our Society and it would be a great pity if we are compelled to relax our efforts through lack of funds.

Mr. Hamilton spoke from the point of view of the horticulturist, Mr. Spence from a knowledge of the struggle of the Association to carry on, Mr. Payne with a view to a permanent organization, and Dr. Powell from observations of bird life extending over the period since 1877. Miss Durand added that a "little boost" from the Government would encourage the Association to persevere in its efforts and mark approval of them.

The Minister promised consideration of this appeal.

The thanks of the Association are warmly extended to Miss Newman, teller of the Dominion Bank, for so efficiently and kindly taking the Box Office at the Hobson lecture, and to Mrs. C. A. Simmons, President, and the young ladies, members of the Commodore Jarvis Chapter of the Navy League, who so graciously acted as ushers at the lecture.

The Secretary's personal thanks are especially due to Mr. Barton for his unfailing assistance in every emergency and his counsel throughout the year as to the affairs of the Association.

In submitting this report I would repeat that the past year has been the most anxious in our history, for the Secretary, but leaves her only resolute to contend better for our objects,

"For sudden the worst turns the best for the brave."

STATEMENT OF THE ACTING TREASURER
from Nov. 16th, 1917, to Dec. 31st, 1918.
RECEIPTS.

Balance on hand, November, 1917	$ 7 57	
Life membership fees, 3 at $10.00	30 00	
Annual membership fees, 62 at $1.00	62 00	
Sale of pins, including those sent to junior members	10 44	
Ernest Harold Baynes lecture, including grant of $100.00 from Ontario Government	242 00	
W. D. Hobson Lecture	107 25	
Interest . .	80	
		$460 06

EXPENDITURE.

Printing . .	$94 85	
Miss Stewart, Typewriting	6 64	
Postage . .	18 00	
Provincial Secretary, filing annual statement	1 00	
Ernest Harold Baynes Lecture	142 33	
Stationery . .	1 20	
W. D. Hobson Lecture, Convocation Hall	25 99	
W. D. Hobson Lecture, Forresters' Hall	108 47	
		398 48
Balance on hand		$61 58
Accounts Unpaid—		
Mail and Empire	$ 74	
Globe Printing Company	70	
G. R. Anderson	4 00	
Wm. Briggs	19 25	
King Edward Hotel	3 00	
		27 69
		$33 89

I certify that I have examined the books and vouchers of the above Society for the year ending Dec. 31, 1918, and find the same to be true and correct in every respect.

(Signed) GORDON A. BROWN,
Auditor.

Both reports were adopted on motion duly made and carried.

REPORT OF THE SECRETARY OF THE
CANADIAN SOCIETY FOR THE PROTECTION OF BIRDS
for the year 1919
read at the Annual Meeting and Banquet in the
King Edward Hotel, November 21, 1919.

In presenting the 5th annual report of the Association, I must note that it is the first to be given since the terrible war, which absorbed and well-nigh exhausted all our interests and energies, came to an end. While this movement was initiated in October, 1913, it was organized only in December, 1914, and incorporated at the beginning of 1915. Hence the major portion of the movement has taken place in Canada under abnormal conditions, and against insurmountable difficulties. For comparatively few persons during these years have recognized the value of birds in their important relation to food production and supported the work. But the Association has not been idle in any of these years, and has been vigorously applying itself to carrying out the objects for which it was incorporated.

The reports already issued, those of 1915, '16 and '17, show that a considerable response from the public, particularly from teachers, met the early distribution of the literature of the Association. Our posters reached thousands of Ontario schools, and thousands of applications for "a book about birds" were received by the Secretary, who, to her regret, was utterly unable to comply with the oft-repeated request. We had no book of popular appeal, illustrated and so forth, to distribute, and this was at last recognized, and in many centres children and teachers have joined the Audubon Society of the United States, which has a rich and varied equipment of literature with which to attract members.

The report of 1918 will be enclosed under cover with the present report when it is printed. It will show that a strong deputation from the Association waited upon the Hon. the Minister of Public Works in December (1918) and made an application for a grant of $1,000. The Government was pleased to give the Association half of this amount for the administration of the work of the Society.

The office at 153 University Avenue has also been generously continued, but telephone service was withdrawn a year ago.

The junior campaign of 1917, conducted through the Anglican juvenile publications, "The Young Soldier" and "Crusader," had been so successful, that a similar effort was attempted through the juvenile Presbyterian publications, so far with much smaller results. But several hundred children have applied for membership. "The Boy Builder," the organ of the Boy's Work Department of the Y. M. C. A., has begun a campaign along the same lines at the request of the Secretary. It is possible we may be able to enlist the interest of other denominational juvenile publications.

It is almost useless, however, to conduct a campaign to interest juniors without a supply of attractive illustrated literature to send them when their interest has been engaged. Children demand the concrete. They want the picture of the bird described before them—and a large picture of it, too.

The Association organized two admirable lectures last winter in the auditorium of the Y. M. C. A., one kindly given by Prof. A. P. Coleman on "Sea Birds," the second kindly given by Prof. E. W. Walker on "Insect Life in Relation to Birds." Both lectures were finely illustrated.

As nothing was doing in the summer vacation, the Secretary organized an open air lecture on the lawn at "Oaklands" by kind consent of the mistress of that estate, on August 18. The Parks Commissioner, Ottawa, and the Dominion Geological Survey loaned a set of lantern slides and a film of bird life for the event. Prof. G. A. Cornish, University of Toronto, assisted the Secretary in giving the entertainment, Dr. John Noble graciously acted as chairman for the evening, while Miss Newman (Dominion Bank) and Miss Joseph unselfishly acted as gatekeepers. The Secretary is very grateful to these generous friends of the Society for their co-operation. The committee of members who supported the project were as follows:— Mrs. C. A. Simmons, Miss Ewan, Mr. Kanagy and Mr. J. Cruso, Treasurer. His statement is as follows:

OAKLANDS LECTURE, AUG. 20, 1919.

Receipts.

By sale of tickets (at 25 cts.) and gate receipts	$32 25

Disbursements.

Wells Brothers, operators	$35 00	
Advertising—Mail	2 88	
Globe	2 86	
Telegram	1 48	
Star	2 00	
World	1 34	
Express charges on slides	90	
Motor car charges	2 50	
"Oaklands" man for attendance	2 00	
Eaton Drug Co. for 34 slides	24 50	
		$75 46
Deficit		$43 21

Tickets and posters were kindly contributed by R. G. McLean, Lombard St.

The seats were kindly loaned by the Board of Education.

The Secretary paid the entire deficit.   J. Cruso, Treasurer.

The bird sanctuary movement is extending, and this year the grounds of the Toronto Golf Club have been established as a wild bird reserve and a number of nesting boxes erected through the efforts of Mr. Frank Payne.

A Dominion-wide campaign has been carried on with the co-operation of the Canadian press in the publication of an article by the Secretary entitled "Food Production and Bird Protection." This has awakened interest and secured members at such widely-separated points as Prince Edward Island and Edmonton.

Meanwhile the distribution of our pamphlets and posters has gone on steadily.

The Association kindled the flourishing Quebec Society for the Protection of Birds two years ago, and this year has encouraged the establishment of the Hamilton Bird Protection Society, a local organization, but a vigorous offshoot of our efforts, which promises to outstrip its parent.

A great step forward was accomplished this year in bird protection in Canada by the Act of the Legislature of Quebec in March, establishing bird sanctuaries on the cliffs of Bonaventure Island, the bird rocks of the Magdalen Islands, and on Perce Rock, Gaspe, thus terminating a disgraceful state of things, in which the beautiful sea birds nesting on these rocks had been cruelly persecuted.

During the autumn of the present year (1919) the Secretary has conducted junior classes in bird study in the Allen Theatre on several Saturday mornings through the generous co-operation of the management of the Theatre, attended with much success.

The most outstanding work projected during the year has been the idea of one of our vice-presidents, Mr. Charles G. Fraser, namely, the Junior Bird-lovers' Clubs.

All of which is submitted.

LAURA B. DURAND, A.A.O.U.,

Secretary.

TREASURER'S REPORT
From 1st January, 1919, to 21st November, 1919.
RECEIPTS.

To Balance from 1918	$61	58
Ontario Government Grant	500	00
Patrons . .	200	00
Life Membership Fees	90	15
Annual Membership Fees	110	00
Sale Pins	20	17
Bank Interest	2	77
		$984 67

EXPENSES.

By Resolution, for administration of office to Secretary....	$583	31
Printing and Stationery.	107	55
Postage . .	30	00
Typing . .	15	20
Cost of Social (25 Oct.)	15	68
Advertising . .	16	12
Lantern Service	8	00
Buttons . .	9	50
Sundries . .	6	30
		$791 66
		$193 01
21 November, To Balance in Bank		$193 01

I have examined the Receipts and Vouchers from Jan. 1st, 1919, to Nov. 8th, 1919, together with the Bank Pass Book, showing a balance in Bank of one hundred and ninety-three dollars and one cent, which is correct in every detail.

G. H. BROWN.

Dec. 5th, 1919.

On motion of Mr. Barton, seconded by Mrs. J. A. C. Cameron, and carried, the reports of the Secretary, Miss Durand, and of the Treasurer, Mr. C. H. Anderson were adopted.

PATRONS:
Mrs. J. A. C. Cameron.
Mrs. W. J. Hanna.

HONORARY MEMBERS:
Hon. F. G. Macdiarmid.
Hon. R. A. Pyne.

LIFE MEMBERS:
Enrolled in 1915 from the unincorporated Society of the same name,
without further fee, having paid $5.00.

Dr. C. K. Clarke ....Toronto
Laura B. Durand .... "
Helen M. Merrill .... "
J. Harry Fleming ....
Joseph Nason ....
Frank Denton .... "
Mrs. Lila M. Cameron (Obit.) ....Meaford
Mrs. Allen Baines (Obit.) ....Toronto

Elected by the Executive of the Incorporated Society 1915-1917.

Frank F. Payne ....Toronto
John D. Spence .... "
James S. Wallace .... "
Samuel Jardine ....
Mrs. Beverley MacInnes (Obit.) ....
Dr. W. H. B. Aikens ....
Mrs. W. H. B. Aikens ....
Miss Elizabeth Dempster ....
Miss Joan Dempster ....
Mrs. C. K. Clarke ....
Mr. L. Clark Macklem (Obit.) ....
Mrs. L. Clark Macklem ....
Francis V. Johns ....
A. H. U. Colquhoun ....
Miss Emily L. Merritt ....
Miss Bessie Baldwin ....
Dr. John M. Baldwin ....
Mrs. John M. Baldwin ....
H. P. Eckardt ....
J. A. C. Cameron ....
Hon. Justice W. R. Riddell ....
Edward B. Brown, K.C. ....
Miss Martin ....
Hon. Sir Wm. Mulock ....
Mrs. Eugene Beaupré ....
V. H. E. Hutcheson ....
Sir John C. Eaton ....
Lady Eaton ....
Mrs. J. J. Gibbons ....
Mrs. F. T. James ....
W. A. McLean .... "
Mrs. R. W. Leonard .... St. Catharines
Sir John Hendrie, K.C.M.G. ....Toronto
Miss Madeline Massey ....East Toronto
Mrs. Harold Tovell .... "
Ralph Horsey (Obit.) ....Agincourt
Mrs. W. C. Harvey ....Toronto
Dr. James Musgrave .... "
Mrs. R. L. Brereton (Obit.) .... "
Mrs. R. W. Thomas .... "
L. A. De Wolfe ....Truro, N.S.

Elected under new tariff of $10, 1918-20.

Miss Barbara Ewan ....Toronto
Mrs. W. T. Moore ....Meaford
Miss Grace˙ James ....Toronto
Mrs. C. A. Simmons .... "
James H. Schofield, M.P.P. ....Trail, B.C.
Prof. E. W. Walker ....Toronto
Miss M. V. McCormick, "Oaklands" .... "
Mr. D. A. Dunlap ....
Mrs. D. A. Dunlap .... "
Moffat Dunlap ....
Mr. R. Owen Merriman ....Hamilton
Mr. R. J. Dilworth ....Toronto
Mr. M. R. Jennings ....Edmonton, Alta.
Dr. N. A. Powell ....Toronto
Edward Cronyn .... "
Dr. J. A. Campbell ....

11

EXECUTIVE OFFICERS, 1920.

President: Frank F. Payne;

Vice-Presidents: Dr. N. A. Powell and
      Principal C. G. Fraser;

Secretary: Miss L. B. Durand, A.A.O.U.;

Treasurer: C. H. Anderson;

Directors: The above officers and
      Hon. Manning Doherty,
      Mrs. Manning Doherty,
      Dr. C. K. Clarke,
      J. D. Spence,
      J. A. C. Cameron,
      Mrs. J. A. C. Cameron,
      Miss Barbara Ewan,
      T. Herbert Barton,
      T. W. Kidd,
      D. A. Dunlap.

CPSIA information can be obtained
at www.ICGtesting.com
Printed in the USA
BVHW091240261118
534010BV00012B/177/P